THE DESPERATE GOURMET

· · · · · · · · · · · · · · · ·

· THE ·

DESPERATE GOURMET

· ·

LOIS SCHENCK

ST. MARTIN'S PRESS NEW YORK

Design by Jaye Zimet

Library of Congress Cataloging-in-Publication Data

Schenck, Lois.
    The desperate gourmet / Lois Schenck.
       p.   cm.
    ISBN 0-312-02191-7 (pbk.)
    1. Quick and easy cookery.   2. Entertaining.   3. Menus.
I. Title.
TX652.S336   1988
641.5′12—dc19   88-11559
                                                                      CIP

                           First Edition
                  10 9 8 7 6 5 4 3 2 1

THIS BOOK IS DEDICATED

TO ANDREW, who graciously starved while his wife was writing a gourmet cookbook . . .

TO TIMOTHY AND MATTHEW, who put up with their mother's "weird food" when what they really wanted was hamburgers . . .

TO MY MOTHER, who always produced a feast for drop-in guests when there was nothing in the house . . .

TO MY GRANDMOTHER, who never believed you *couldn't* do it all . . .

AND TO MY FRIENDS, most of whom have given up cooking!